Includes Five SAT Words to Know
MEETS STATE AND NATIONAL STANDARDS
Africa
A Safari Through Its Amazing Nations!
IT'S YOUR WORLD
LIVE WORK PLAY LEARN
Where Do You Want to Go?
Hey! It's the Masai Mara! Do you want to go?
TIME ZONE • CULTURE • CUSTOMS • CLOTHING • HIST
FOOD • CULTURE • CUSTOMS • CLOTHING • HISTORY • LANDMARKS
By Carole Marsh

Live • Work • Play • Learn

GALLOPADE INTERNATIONAL

Gallopade International is introducing SAT words that kids need to know in our books. The SAT words in this book have a gray box around them. Students can look up the definitions and increase their vocabulary. Happy Learning!

Gallopade is proud to be a member and supporter of these educational organizations and associations:

Association for the Study of African American Life and History
National Alliance of Black School Educators
American Booksellers Association
American Library Association
International Reading Association
National Association for Gifted Children
The National School Supply and Equipment Association
The National Council for the Social Studies
Museum Store Association
Association of Partners for Public Lands
Association of Booksellers for Children

At the time of publication, all websites referenced in this document were valid. However, due to the changing nature of the Internet, some addresses may change or the content become less relevant.

It's Your World Books

Africa: A Safari Through Its Amazing Nations!

Australia: The Land Down Under for Mates of All Ages!

Canada: The Maple Leaf Melting Pot Country!

China: A Great Wall Runs Thru It!

Egypt: An Ancient Land of Lore; a Modern Land of Oil and More!

France: The Ooh-La-La Country Everyone Loves!

Germany: The Country of Fairytale Castles and Cutting Edge Science!

Greece: A Volcanic Land of Ancient Olympic Origins!

India: Land of Six Senses and Intriguing Mystery!

Italy: The Country of Amazing Fountains and Awesome Arts!

Japan: An Island Country of Endless Intrigue!

Mexico: A Colorful Land of Exotic Culture!

Middle East: Ancient Countries of Current Events Headlines!

Russia: The Great Bear and Its Dramatic History!

South America: A Continent of Countries of Amazing Proportions!

United Kingdom: The Country of Ships, Sealing Wax, Cabbages, and Kings!

Other Carole Marsh Related Titles:

The Mystery of the Ancient Pyramid

The Rip-Roaring Mystery on the African Safari

Table of Contents

A Letter from the Author

From the desk of CAROLE MARSH

Hey kids,

It's your world! It really, really is!

Of course, you already know that, don't you? You surf the 'net, listen to satellite radio, watch television shows and movies set all around the globe–kids today are much more "worldly" than in the past, and that's a good thing!

Now's a great time to learn something about another part of the world–such as Africa. Why? Because one day, you might actually visit there (if you have not already!). You might go to school there–many colleges have ties with international schools around the globe. You might even go on to work in a foreign country!

Many companies have positions in other countries. Companies are "going global" as fast as they can. They have branch offices, manufacturing plants, and customer service centers scattered around the globe!

So, ready or not: YOU are a Citizen of the World! And you'll want to be a good one. How do you do that? You'll find out everything you can about that country, how it's the same, and how it's different from your own country. What language is spoken there? What customs do the people observe? What foods do they enjoy? What do they do for fun? What has happened in this part of the world, and what is happening there now? It's fun... and the more you learn, the more you will enjoy whatever global opportunity comes your way!

This book is a good place to start your learning journey– so take advantage of the world– IT'S YOUR WORLD, after all ... and guess what? It's a BIG world, after all!

Happy traveling and learning,

Carole Marsh
Always with passport in hand!

Why Should We Care About Africa?

Africa is a land like no other. The human race got its start in Africa! It is the second largest continent on earth! It is three times the size of the United States! Africa's 52 countries offer amazing attractions. Africa has rainforests and grasslands, plus lions, impala, and elephants. Africa is home to the biggest desert in the world, the Sahara!

Middle Eastern countries like Egypt, Libya, and Algeria, are part of Africa, too. Most of the world's oil comes from that part of the world (and you know how much we all need oil!). The continent also produces half the world's diamonds and gold.

One day, you might visit Africa to go on a safari in Tanzania, swim in the Indian Ocean, or tour a diamond mine in South Africa! It could happen!

Write home about it! Write a postcard to your family telling about your trip to Africa!

Top Fast Africa Facts!

Important facts to remember about the continent of Africa:

- Three-fourths of Africa is in the tropics. It is the world's most tropical continent.
- It is the second largest continent after Asia.
- There are 54 countries in Africa.
- Africa is the world's poorest continent.
- There are more than 1,000 different languages in Africa.
- The largest city in Africa is Cairo.
- Africa was home to one of the world's first great civilizations, the Egyptian Empire.
- Kilimanjaro, one of the world's largest mountains, is actually a volcano.
- The word "safari" originated in Africa and it is Swahili for "journey."
- Africa has the largest (African Elephant), the fastest (Cheetah), and the tallest (Giraffe) mammals on land.
- The most popular tourist destination in Africa is Egypt.

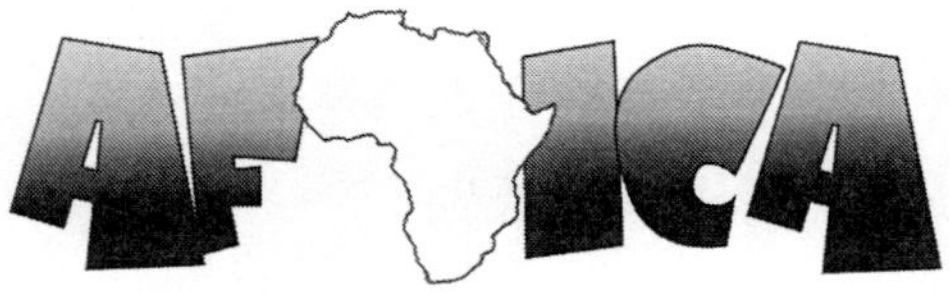

Now, you figure out the rest!

1. The largest city in Africa is __ __ __ __ __.

2. Kilimanjaro is a mountain and a __ __ __ __ __ __ __.

3. The word __ __ __ __ __ __ means "journey."

4. After __ __ __ __, Africa is the second largest continent.

5. The cheetah is the __ __ __ __ __ __ __ land mammal in the world.

Where in the World Is Africa?

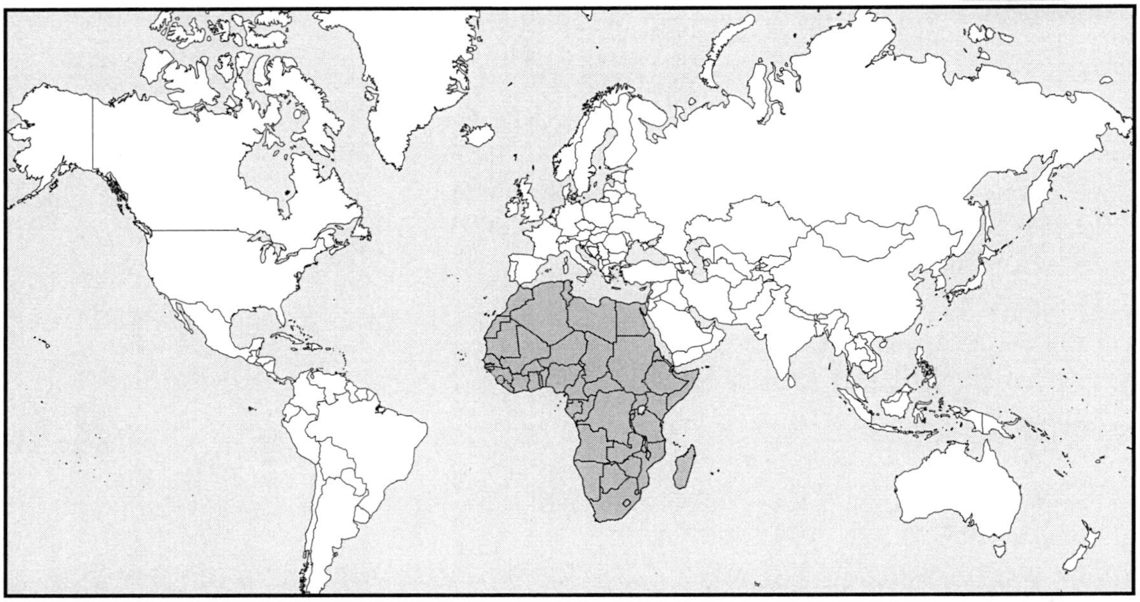

- Africa is one of the seven continents, located south of Europe and west of Asia.
- Africa is the second largest continent on Earth.
- The Sahara Desert covers the northern African countries. Be sure to bring your own water because it's hot and dry!
- Mt. Kilimanjaro rises 5,895 meters (19,340 feet) above sea level and is a favorite site for mountain-climbing tourists.
- Madagascar is the world's fourth-largest island. (Have you seen the movie?)
- More than 1,000 languages are spoken across the African continent.
- The equator cuts through the countries of Gabon, the Republic of the Congo, the Democratic Republic of the Congo, Uganda, Kenya, and Somalia.
- The west coast country of Liberia means "liberty," and was settled by former African American slaves.
- The world's longest river, the Nile, is in Africa.
- Africa is almost an island. Its only connection to other land is the tiny Sinai Peninsula in Egypt.

Do You Know?

1. Russia, Canada, and China are the only countries bigger than this African desert.

   a. Kalahari b. Sahara c. Namib d. None of these

2. The ocean that lies to the west of Africa is:

   a. Southern b. Pacific c. Indian d. Atlantic

The Slave Trade

A slave is someone who belongs to another person and has no rights of their own. Can you imagine being someone's slave?

Between 1440 and 1880, 12 million Africans were sold into slavery and taken from their native homeland. Some were taken as war prisoners. Others were kidnapped. Most slaves were captured by fellow Africans. They were sold to Europeans and Americans who needed workers for their plantations and mines in the New World. African slave traders negotiated with African kings and merchants along the western coast. They traded beads, shells, fabric, horses, and guns in exchange for human lives.

Only the healthiest Africans were taken as slaves because the journey was so dangerous. Some died on the long march to the African coast. Others died in camps waiting to be shipped. Half of the slaves who made it to the ships died on the terrible voyage across the Atlantic Ocean.

The slave trade had long-lasting consequences for African society. Slave traders took young adult males, so families fell apart, and villages were left without their leaders and workers for generations.

Crosswords!

Use your new knowledge to fill in the crossword puzzle.

Across

4. With the males gone,villages were left without ___________.

6. From 1440 to 1880, the Atlantic _____ _____ flourished. (2 words)

Down

1. Some people became slaves as _______ of war.

2. The numbers who died were well into the ______.

3. Negotiations were made with African kings and ____________.

5. Slaves were needed in the ______ ______ (2 words) to work on plantations.

The Amazing History of Africa!

Africa is home to some of the world's earliest civilizations! From the most primitive of hunting and gathering tribes to Egypt, the continent's first kingdom, Africa has had a tremendous role in human history.

After the Egyptian empire reached its peak, conquerors from Asia, Europe, and the Roman Empire colonized Africa. Early western conquerors were interested only in the African countries along the Mediterranean Sea, because they were easier to get to. Crossing the Sahara desert seemed impossible until the Arabs invaded!

European powers have always had their hold on Africa. Several European countries divided the African continent. The Berlin Conference was organized in 1884 to control colonization and trade in Africa.

During the 1950s and 1960s, most African nations became independent. Many of the newly independent states failed because of dishonesty by their leaders and the AIDS epidemic. Today, Africa is plagued by poverty. But countries like Botswana have found successful ways to manage their money. They serve as role models of hope for other African nations.

Timeline!
Number these events in the order that they took place, first to last.

____ The Berlin Conference

____ The Egyptian Empire

____ African Nations gain Independence

____ Europe dominates Africa

____ Botswana adopts successful economics

____ The Arab invasion

Famous African Folks!

Matching!

Match these famous African people with their accomplishments.

____ 1. "I spent 27 years as a political prisoner in South Africa before becoming the country's first black president in 1994. I was jailed for opposing the government's policy of racial separation, known as apartheid. I won the Nobel Peace Prize in 1993."

____ 2. "An Anglican Archbishop, I received the 1984 Nobel Peace Prize for my nonviolent work against apartheid. During the 1970s and 1980s, I led a campaign against a government ban on anti-apartheid demonstrations."

____ 3. "As the king of Mali from 1312 to 1337 C.E., I made my empire a world power. My greatest contribution to Mali history was spreading its fame and reputation to other lands. I established Islam as the official state religion to unite the tribes."

____ 4. "I performed the world's first human heart transplant on December 3, 1967. My patient, a 53-year-old dentist named Louis Washkansky, survived for 18 days."

____ 5. "I am one of two musicians credited with modernizing makossa, a type of music. My song *Soul Makossa* contains the chant, "mamako, mamasa, maka makossa," which Michael Jackson used in *Wanna Be Startin' Somethin.*"

____ 6. "A South African explorer, I am best known for circling the planet along the equator without any motorized transport. I hiked, swam, canoed, biked, and sailed 29,000 miles."

A. Manu Dibango

B. Mansa Musa

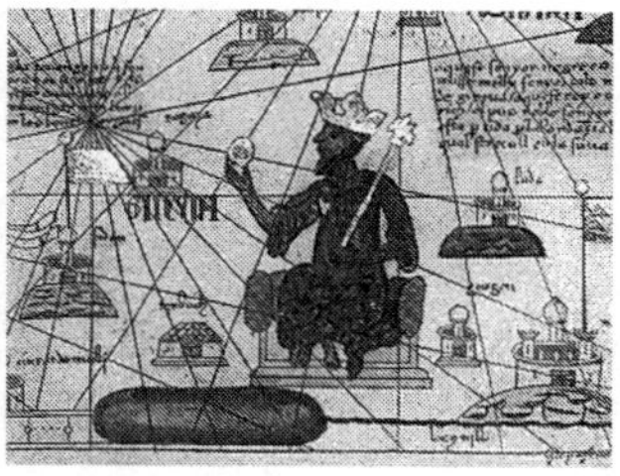

C. Nelson Mandela

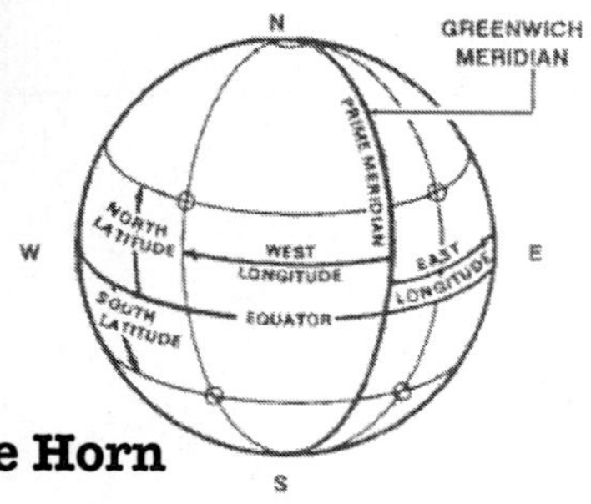

D. Mike Horn

E. Desmond Tutu

F. Christiaan Barnard

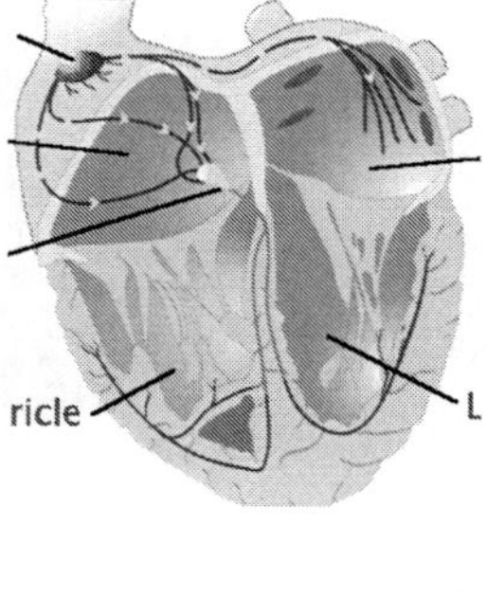

Guts and Glory African Style!

A. This disease has caused vast amount of suffering through sickness and death. It has destroyed families, schools, workplaces, and the continent's economy.

B. This serious food shortage affects millions of people in Africa. It leaves poor people, especially kids, in a state of starvation. Without rain, crops can't grow, and animals and human beings can't live.

C. Some large exotic animals in Africa face extinction because the government allows hunters to kill endangered species. Often referred to as the "Big Five," the African elephant, black rhinoceros, lion, leopard, and Cape buffalo are the most dangerous animals to track on foot.

D. The government blocked the education of black people. But this person worked hard in school. He adopted a policy known as the "Black Consciousness" to help people struggling under this unfair system.

E. These tropical storms bring powerful hurricanes and floods. They begin in the ocean. Islands like Madagascar often find themselves in their path of destruction.

Mixed Up!
Match the paragraph to the word the paragraph describes.

CYCLONES ____

____ **AIDS**

STEPHEN BIKO ____

FAMINE AND DROUGHT ____

BIG GAME HUNTS ____

Masked!

African masks are said to be magical! Many African tribes believe that masks possess the spirits of their ancestors, animals, and other powerful beings. Masks that represent harmful spirits are used to gain power.

The mask is an art form that dates back to the earliest civilizations in Africa. Masks are made from wood, clay, leather, metal, and fabric. The construction of masks and their use are unique to each tribe.

Masks are important to African culture and tradition. They are objects of family pride. Throughout history, masks have been used in ceremonies, celebrations, harvesting, preparing for war, and for religious purposes.

Over time, rituals and ceremonies using masks have become less common in Africa. Today, masks can be found on display in museums and galleries throughout the world.

The many faces of you!
Get creative. Fill in the face in this mask to represent yourself. Are you ferocious and brave like the spirit of a lion, or are you as powerful and strong as the African elephant?

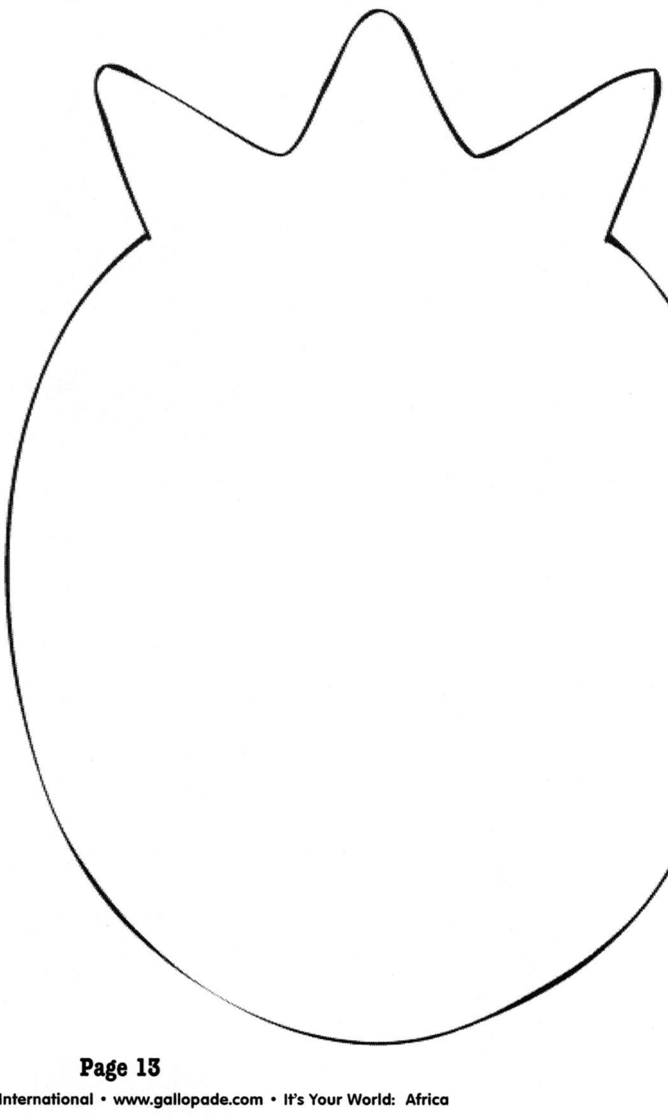

Changed by Chimps!

Jane Goodall

How would you like to hang out with chimpanzees? Jane Goodall has done just that—for 45 years! Goodall has spent much of her life studying Gombe chimpanzees in East Africa. What she discovered has forever changed the way people view primates.

Unlike most scientists, Goodall gave the chimps names instead of numbers. At first, the chimpanzees were afraid of her, but she slowly gained their confidence. The first chimp to touch Goodall was a baby she named Fifi. Today, that chimp is the mother of eight and a grandmother.

Goodall watched chimps make tools. She noticed that they go on dates and have lasting family relationships. She even witnessed one chimp family adopt an orphan into its group. She also discovered that, like humans, chimps engage in brutal warfare. She tracked a four-year war in which a dominant group wiped out members of another group.

Goodall also runs an orphanage for chimpanzees whose mothers were killed by poachers (people hunting illegally). Through her work, she hopes young people will have the compassion to improve the environment for all living things.

Note: Chimpanzees are not meant to be domesticated animals. Jane Goodall lived with them in their natural environment.

Word Fun!

The Gombe chimps didn't use words to express themselves but you do! Use the letters of Jane Goodall's name to create as many words with three letters or more as you can.

Jane Goodall

Victoria Falls, A Site to See!

Victoria Falls is the largest waterfall in the world! Africans call it "the smoke that thunders." It is located in southern Africa on the Zambezi River between the countries of Zambia and Zimbabwe. The unusual form of Victoria Falls enables virtually the whole width of the falls to be viewed face-on. The falls are part of two national parks and draw many tourists to the area.

The falls are approximately twice as wide and twice as deep as Niagara Falls.

The gorge that exits the falls is great for white water rafting.

The loud roar produced by the falls can be heard from a distance of about 25 miles.

In November 1855, the falls were made known to the outside world by David Livingstone, a British explorer.

The falls were named after Britain's Queen Victoria.

Create your very own travel pamphlet.
Concentrate on an area that interests you. Perhaps you enjoyed learning about the people. Or maybe it was the animals that interested you. Fold a piece of paper into three sections. This will give you six areas on which to put information.

Gentlemen First!

Customs and culture vary widely from country to country. Sometimes they vary in different regions of the same country. Here are custom and cultural differences observed by the countries that make up the African continent!

- Greetings last a long time in most African countries. It is polite to shake hands for several minutes and to ask about a person's family, work, and even the weather.
- In many African countries, men and women eat separately. The men eat first, followed by the women.
- The left hand is considered unclean in most African countries. You must only use your right hand when shaking hands, offering a gift, or eating.
- In Kenya, beverages are not served with a meal, since it is considered impolite to eat and drink at the same time.
- In several African countries, people drive on the left side of the road. That's opposite from the United States!
- People from Muslim countries celebrate the Ramadan holiday by fasting (not eating) during the day, and feasting from sunset to the early morning.
- In South Africa, a person's 21st and 40th birthdays are celebrated with huge parties.
- In Senegal, it is polite to avoid eye contact when talking to someone who is older or more senior.

Create your own!

Customs and cultural activities can help define who we are. Think about your family and friends and come up with some new customs for everyone to try.

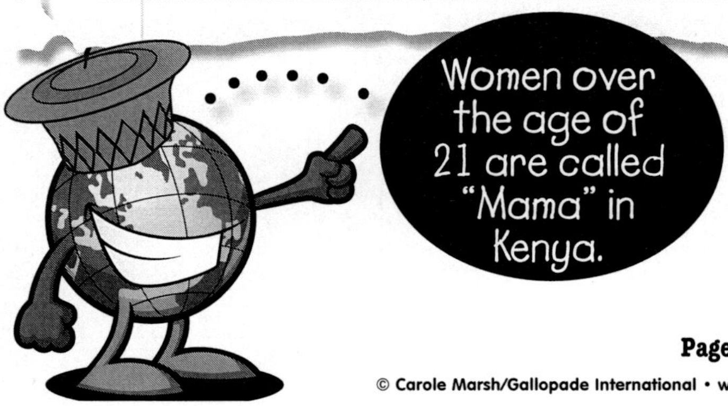

They Say What?

There are many languages spoken in Africa, such as Swahili, French, English, Portuguese, Setswana, and Amharic.

Match it up!
Below are some common Swahili phrases or words. See if you can match them to the English word.

hodi	child
mtoto	hello
baba	cat
mama	no
ramani	family
paka	blue
mbwa	mother
siyo	dog
bluu	map
familia	father

Happy Holidays!

The countries that make up the continent of Africa celebrate many holidays and festivals. In West Africa, most of the countries celebrate **New Year's** on January 1st. They also observe **Labor Day**—a day that celebrates and honors workers—on May 1st, just as many other nations around the world do.

Because both Christianity and Islam are practiced in Africa, many countries celebrate important holidays of both religions. For example, **Christmas Day** and **Easter** are observed by most West African countries. These same countries also celebrate **Eid-al-Fitr**, the end of the holy month of Ramadan. During **Ramadan**, Muslims fast (go without eating) during daylight hours.

Many of the African nations also celebrate an **Independence Day** to celebrate the end of colonial reign. The date is different for each nation. Many countries celebrate with a mixture of traditional and modern customs. Traditional clothing may be worn, but the people will be listening to modern music, or traditional food is eaten, but there is a fireworks show.

Write it down!
Pretend you are visiting Africa. Write a letter to your best friend. Tell him or her about African Independence Day. Describe how it is different from ours. Describe how it is the same.

Africa on the Stage and in the Museums!

The arts culture in Africa is as vast as the Sahara Desert. African people use art and music in religious rituals and ceremonies to communicate with the spiritual world.

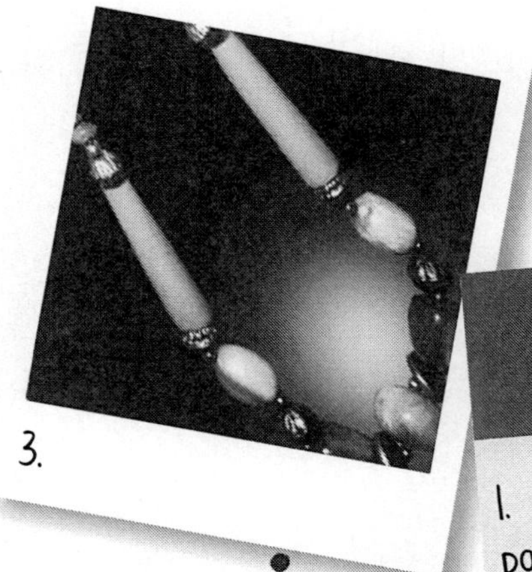

3.

Notes

1. African masks are dramatic portraits of spirit beings and departed relatives.

2. A figure in tribal carving may represent an ancestor destined to stand in a shrine.

3. African culture places great emphasis on appearance, so jewelry has received vast attention for centuries.

4. African folklore paintings incorporate amazing richness and variety of colors.

5. Music is essential to African storytelling tradition. Before selecting any instrument, consideration is given to its dramatic power.

2.

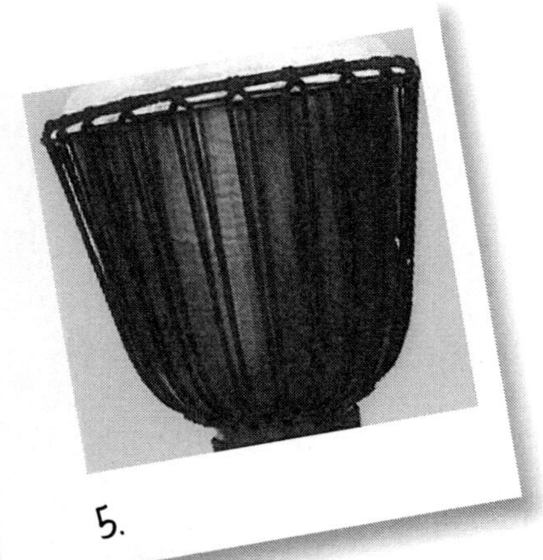

5.

1.

4.

What's for Dinner?

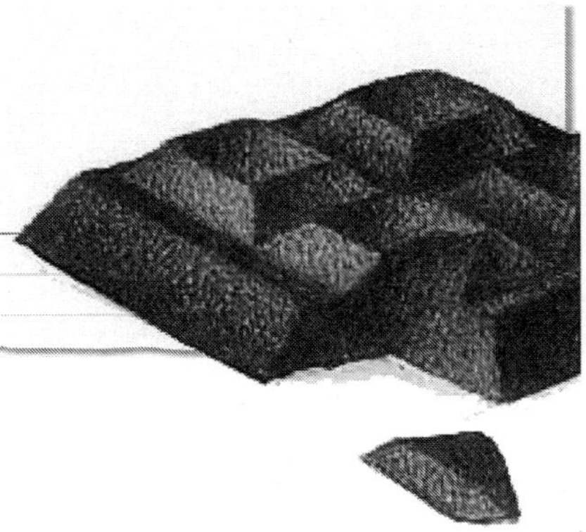

The continent of Africa enjoys a wide variety of diets and dishes. For instance, countries along the coast enjoy a diet consisting mainly of fish. Colonization had a major influence on the cuisine of Africa. Check out the different kinds of foods you may find in Africa.

Couscous is a North African dish made of crushed grain that is steamed and served with lamb or chicken in a spicy sauce.

Piripiri are hot pepper dishes found in Mozambique.

Berbere is a red pepper spice used in Ethiopia.

Foofoo is a yam, corn, and plantain pudding.

RECIPE

Always ask an adult for help when cooking!

Injera

mmmmmmmm...this was good!

INGREDIENTS

1 cup whole wheat flour
1 cup unbleached white flour
1/2 teaspoon baking soda
2 cups club soda

DIRECTIONS

1. Combine flour and baking soda in a large bowl.
2. Add club soda, stir well to form a thin batter.
3. Heat a large, well-seasoned or non-stick griddle until hot. Brush lightly with oil.
4. Using a large cup or ladle, begin on the outside of the griddle and pour in a circle around the inside edges until the center is filled in. Quickly tilt the griddle back and forth to fill in any holes and spread evenly. Cook for 1-2 minutes, until surface is spongy and filled with tiny air bubbles. Do not flip the bread - just slide off griddle onto a large plate.
5. Continue cooking injera until all batter is used, transferring them to the plate as they are done. Arrange them around the outside edges of the plate so that the center overlaps.
6. Serve immediately with a meat or vegetable stew.

Makes 6 large rounds.

South African Fun!

People everywhere love to play games! Africans enjoy a game called jukskei. This 200-year-old sport developed in South Africa. The object of the game is to knock over a peg that is planted in a sandpit.

Jukskei is usually played in teams of four. Every member gets to throw two wooden pins known as skeis. Each time a team member knocks over the peg, that person gets three points. If the peg isn't knocked out, the team with the skei lying closest to the peg scores as many points as it has skeis closer to the peg than its opponent's closest skei. The first team to get exactly 23 points wins. If a team gets more than 23 points, it starts again from zero.

Figure it out!
Figure out the answers to these questions about jukskei.

The Australian team plays against India at the 2004 One Day International cricket match.

1. If a jukskei playing field is 16 meters long, how many playing fields would fit down the length of a football field, which is 91.44 meters? How many would fit across the width of a football field, which is 48.8 meters? (Round to the lowest whole number.)

____

2. Africans have played jukskei since 1743. How many months have they played jukskei?

____

Fast Fact:
Jukskei is said to date back to 1734 in South Africa. Bored transport riders passing the time planted a stick in the ground to see who could hit it from a distance with one of the pins from the oxen yokes.

South Africa's new government launched the Indigenous Games Project in 2001, which identified jukskei as one of seven indigenous games that should be encouraged and developed.

Golden City!

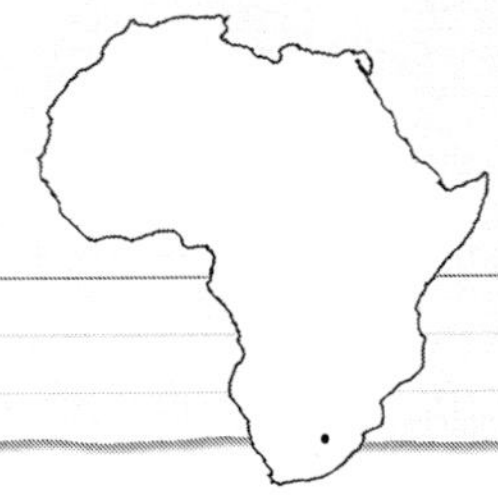

Since the beginning of civilization, men have sought that shiny precious metal called gold! Johannesburg, South Africa is known for its gold mines. Its nickname is "Egoli," which means "place of gold." When gold was discovered in the area in 1886, flocks of gold diggers and fortune hunters arrived to find their fortune!

Johannesburg has been rebuilt four times. First it was a tented camp, then a collection of tin shacks, then a town of four-story British brick buildings, and finally a city of modern skyscrapers!

In 1900, during the Boer War, the British occupied Johannesburg. They began a system of racial separation that eventually became known as apartheid. Since the end of apartheid, blacks have moved into formerly all-white districts in the central city and inner suburbs.

Today, Johannesburg is the economic and cultural center of South Africa. "Joburg" is a dynamic city with hotels, a planetarium, parks, the Nelson Mandela Bridge, and Telkom Joburg Tower. The Apartheid Museum is the city's main tourist attraction.

True or False?

Read the following statements. Write T for True and F for False.

Just 117 years ago Johannesburg was a dusty, rocky, barren grassland. Today it is a man-made urban forest with six million trees.

1. ___ People have always been able to live anywhere they want in Johannesburg.
2. ___ "Egoli" means "place of conceit."
3. ___ In 1886, flocks of geese arrived in Johannesburg.
4. ___ During the Boer War, Johannesburg was occupied by the British.
5. ___ Johannesburg is a dynamic city with museums, parks, and the Brooklyn Bridge.
6. ___ Today, Johannesburg is a man-made urban forest with 6 million trees.

Africa Did It First!

Without Missing a Beat!
The world's first heart transplant was performed by Dr. Christiaan Barnard in Cape Town, South Africa on December 3, 1967.

This CAT Doesn't Meow!
The CAT scan was developed by South African physicist Allan Cormack. It allows doctors to see sharper images of the human body than an x-ray can provide.

That's Not Creepy!
The Kreepy Krauly pool vacuum cleaner, which cleans a pool automatically, was invented by Ferdinand Chauvier in 1951.

Word Fun!

This is fun to do with someone else. Ask a friend for words to substitute for the blanks in the story. Their word substitutions will have a humorous effect when the resulting story is then read aloud.

I want to be the first person to ______________ (ACTION VERB)

across ______________ (COUNTRY)! I've been training for this

since ______________ (MONTH). I'm in ______________ (ADJECTIVE) shape.

My ______________ (ADJECTIVE) adventure will begin on

______________ (FAVORITE HOLIDAY). I won't be hard to miss;

I'll be the one wearing a ______________ (COLOR)

______________ (ARTICLE OF CLOTHING) and a pair of matching

______________ (FOOTWEAR). My faithful friends,

______________ (FAMOUS ATHLETE) and

______________ (CARTOON CHARACTER) will be there to cheer for me.

I'm bringing my ______________ (NOUN) along for good luck.

I'm confident I'll be the first!

Where It Started!
Dr. Louis Leakey, born in Kenya, was credited with proving that mankind descended from Africa.

He Can Dunk Without Jumping!
At seven feet seven inches, Sudan's Manute Bol was the tallest man to ever play in the National Basketball Association

Read It in English!
Leila Abouzeid was the first female author from Morocco to have her work translated from Arabic to English.

On Safari!

Imagine how thrilling it would be to come face to face with a lion, a leopard, an elephant, or a rhinoceros—running free! An African safari is a great way to observe the world's most exotic animals in their natural habitats.

The word "safari" is Swahili for "journey." If you don't like shots, the very first part of your journey will test your courage. Before leaving home you will need to get several vaccinations. Those shots prevent malaria and other diseases spread by mosquitoes and other bugs!

African Safari

A daytime safari in open jeeps or mini buses with a park ranger is the safest way to go. But on a night drive you get to see nocturnal animals like the leopard, laughing hyenas, porcupines, and more! Other safaris are done on foot with an armed guide. You might learn about animal tracks and plant life. You might even get to study some elephant poop! Other types of safaris are conducted by helicopter or balloon, in boats, or on elephants or camels.

Word Fun!

Write 5 questions you would ask your guide if you went on a safari. Ask about facts that are not commonly known. We've given you an example to get started.

Example: Why do male lions have manes?

1. ____?

2. ____?

3. ____?

4. ____?

5. ____?

Separated No More!

"Apartheid" mean "separateness." For hundreds of years the policy of apartheid divided black and white South Africans. Only white citizens were allowed to vote and participate in government. The law decided where members of each racial group could live, the jobs they could hold, and the type of education they could receive.

Black political leaders and peaceful protesters who challenged apartheid were jailed and tortured. Nelson Mandela led a crusade to change the South African government's policy. He was sentenced to life in prison. Mandela refused to give up his fight against apartheid, and he spent nearly 30 years in prison.

In 1990, South African President F.W. de Klerk released Mandela from jail. The two men later shared the Nobel Peace Prize for their role in bringing unity to South Africa. Mandela was elected South Africa's first black president.

The end of apartheid was a great victory for all people in South Africa!

Mandela **de Klerk**
Two men responsible for the end of apartheid

Revealing Answer!

Vilakazi Street in Soweto, South Africa, is the only street in the world that houses two Nobel Prize winners. Nelson Mandela is one. Follow the instructions to reveal the other.

1. Cross off the first and last letters.
2. Cross off any letter "Y."
3. Cross off the letters that represent the Roman numeral 10.
4. Cross off the second "C" from the left.
5. Cross off the third and tenth letters from the right.
6. Cross off the sixth and last letters of the alphabet.

VAYRXCFHZBISCHYOP DYEZSXMFOXNBD TXUYTEUG

Division Was the Wrong Answer!

Europe's interest in Africa didn't end with the slave trade. European countries still wanted Africa's gold, diamonds, and other abundant natural resources. In 1884, European nations met to stake and sort out their claims to African colonies at a meeting called the Berlin West Africa Conference. This process became known as the "Scramble for Africa." The future of Africa was being decided, but there was one big problem—there were no Africans at the conference!

The European division of Africa created big problems. Boundaries were drawn with no concern for traditional boundaries or societies. This caused conflict between tribes and destroyed many African traditions. The Europeans divided Africa to benefit themselves, not Africans.

By the early 1900s, almost all of Africa was under European control. Many Europeans treated the Africans cruelly. They tried to impose a European way of life on Africans, paying no attention to the African way of life. This division of Africa had long-lasting effects on the continent. It is one of the reasons the countries of Africa have so many problems today.

Revealing Answer!

Starting with the first letter, cross off every other letter to reveal one of the countries that did not fall under European control.

I E B T J H V I R O S P L I U A

____

"From Here to Timbuktu"

Why does Timbuktu have a reputation for being a far-away place? Maybe it's because the city is located at the end of the Sahara desert in the West-African nation of Mali. Even today, the city can only be reached by camel and boat. Historically a trading outpost, it was given the status of being an exotic and distant land.

At one time, Timbuktu was an economic and cultural capital. Thriving trade made it a rich city. It was the center of the Trans-Sahara Trade Route. Its closeness to the Niger River made the city a powerful empire that mined salt and gold for trade.

Timbuktu attracted scholars and religious people. It became the intellectual and spiritual center of Islam. Great universities, mosques, and libraries were built, and some remain even today.

Timbuktu lost a lot of money when navigators found another route through the desert, and traders were able to find goods to buy and sell in other countries. In 1591, the Moroccan army invaded Timbuktu, conquering it for their sultan. Timbuktu became a poor country.

Today, instead of merchants and scholars, the Sahara Desert brings only dry wind and drifting sands. This destruction, known as desertification, is a persistent threat to the city's historical buildings, vegetation, and water supply. In 1990, a conservation program began to protect the city.

Did you know?
The idea that Timbuktu is a mythical city has survived to the present day. Some people do not even believe it exists. That's a mystery!

Figure it out!

List the causes of Timbuktu's rise on the left, and on the right, the causes of its fall.

RISE	FALL
1. Thriving ______________	1. New route through ______________
2. Close to ______________ ______________	2. ______________ traded in other countries
3. Mined ______________ and ______________	3. ______________ Army invaded

Fashion Wrap Up!

Have you ever seen an African woman with a colorful wrap on her head? That wrap is called a gele. Originating in Nigeria, the gele symbolizes beauty, wisdom, and elegance.

The quality of the gele and its assembly are an important status symbol. Achieving the perfect look often requires help from a friend. Unlike most head wraps that stay close to the head, the gele is made to stand away from the head. It certainly isn't easy to wear in a car—its two yards of fabric can sit up to 30 inches high!

Traditionally, the gele was made of a hand-loomed cloth by the Yoruba tribe. Fabrics used today usually are stiff to make it easy to assemble. The gele is the most striking piece of the traditional Yoruba woman's outfit!

Dress Up!

Christina is going on a tour of Africa. Below are traditional African outfits. Choose which outfit she will wear. Color the clothing, and draw a line from the piece of clothing to Christina or cut the clothing out and dress her up!

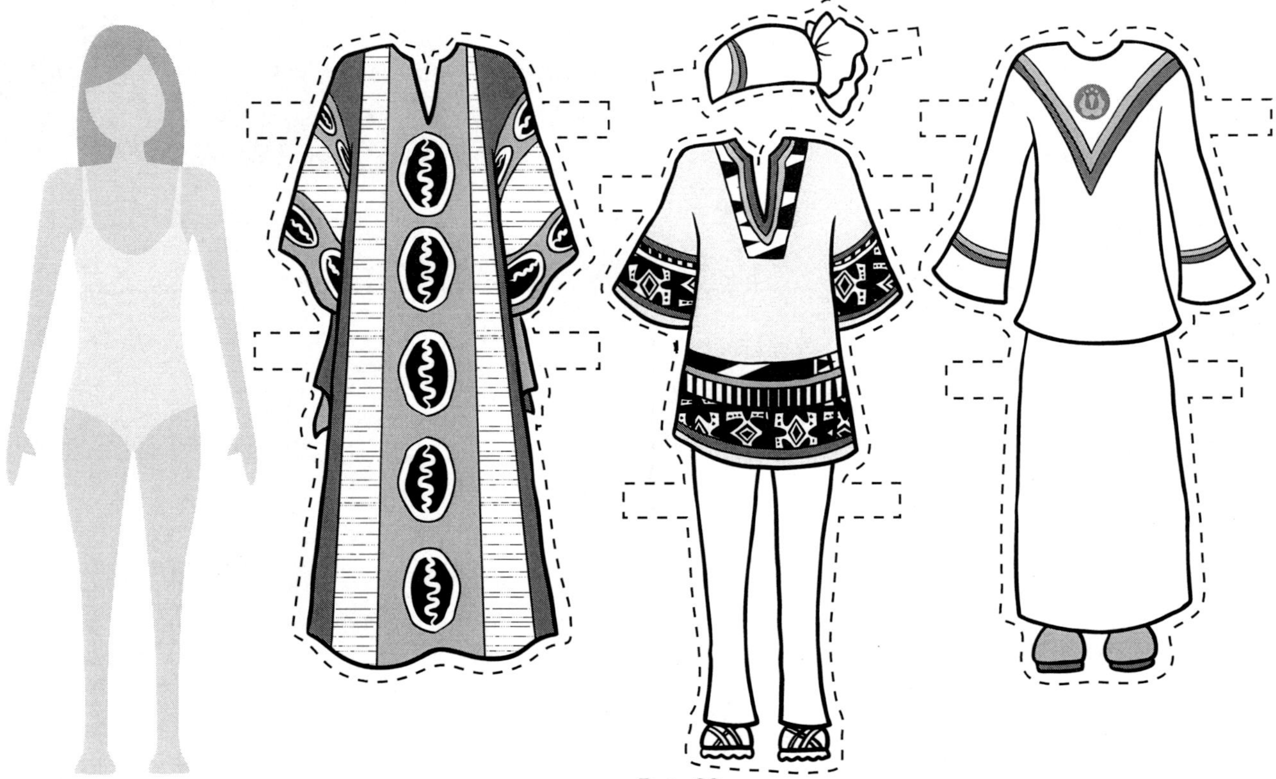

Assorted Architecture!

Figure it out!
Use the following clues to figure out the name of this famous building in Marrakech, Morocco.

- It is one of the most prominent cultural landmarks of the Arab nations.
- The building was designed to have arcades that surround a courtyard.
- It has a minaret, or tall spire, that is decorated with green tile.
- It is a Muslim house of worship and education.
- It is named after the Almoravid amir, a leader of religious and moral reform.
- Much of this great building was destroyed during the Alhomad reign.

As They Say in Africa...

Figure it out!
Here are a few African words you may already know. Why? Because we use them as "English" words all the time!

apartheid: policy of separate development/living

coffee: a stimulant beverage prepared from roasted beans

cola: a beverage usually with caramel coloring that contains caffeine

fandango: a style of folk and flamenco music and dance

gumbo: a stew or soup popular in Louisiana

jamboree: a large gathering of Boy or Girl Scouts, or a festive musical gathering of regional folks

jazz: a popular musical form that originated among African-Americans in New Orleans

jumbo: a very large African bush elephant

Kwanzaa: a holiday honoring African heritage, observed from December 26 to January 1

merengue: a style of Latin American music and dance

mojo: a type of magic charm

mumbo jumbo: an English phrase for a meaningless ritual or nonsense

safari: an overland journey by tourists to Africa traditionally for a big-game hunt

trek: a long, hard journey

zombie: a reanimated human corpse

Further Resources

Further Resources

African Union Headquarters
P.O. Box 3243
Roosvelt Street
W21K19
Addis Ababa, Ethiopia
Phone: (251) 11 551 77 00
Fax: (251) 11 551 78 44
www.africa-union.org

African Tourism Organization
14, Cotton Street Kanifing South, Kombo, St. Mary's
Sere Kunda, The Gambia
Phone: 220 9912432
Fax: 202 223 1261
ato@voladv.org

Zambia National Tourist Board
zntb@zambiatourism.org.zm
http://www.zambiatourism.com

Interesting Websites

http://www.safaris.com/

http://www.saharamet.com/

http://www.tanzaniaparks.com/

http://www.climbingkilimanjaro.com/

http://www.victoriafalls.com/

Answer Key

Page 7
1. Cairo 2. volcano 3. safari
4. Asia 5. fastest

Page 8
1. b 2. d

Page 9
1. prisoners
2. millions
3. merchants
4. leadership
5. New World
6. slave trade

Page 10
4, 1, 5, 3, 6, 2

Page 11
1. C 2. E 3. B 4. F 5. A 6. D

Page 12
Cyclones – E, AIDS – A, Stephen Biko – D,
Famine and Drought – B, Big Game Hunts – C

Page 17
hodi - hello
mtoto - child
baba - father
mama - mother
ramani - map
paka - cat
mbwa - dog
siyo - no
bluu - blue
familia – family

Page 21
1. 5 and 3
2. answers will vary by the current year

Page 22
1. F
2. F
3. F
4. T
5. F
6. F

Page 25
Archbishop Desmond Tutu

Page 26
Ethiopia

Page 27
Rise:
trade
trade route
salt and gold
Fall:
desert
Traders
Moroccan

Page 29
Ali bin Yusuf Mosque